Louis Weber, CEO
Publications International, Ltd.
7373 North Cicero Avenue
Lincolnwood, Illinois 60712

www.pilbooks.com

Permission is never granted for commercial purposes.

Manufactured in China.

8 7 6 5 4 3 2 1

ISBN-13: 978-1-4127-1129-6
ISBN-10: 1-4127-1129-0

Tales From the
Teacher's Lounge

new seasons®

I realized too late that the apple was just a distraction. Once again, I was a victim of the classic tack-on-the-seat trick.

When Timmy's mother came into the classroom with her hair in rollers, he hid his face so she wouldn't see him. Unfortunately, he was wearing that plaid shirt!

The kids stayed in that position until the principal left and we could call the janitor to come and get the paint stain out of the rug.

Lillie counted to 10 on her own hands, but she needed to borrow Jacob's hand to make it to 13.

That little chatterbox had been driving me crazy. The day his backpack got caught on the coat hook, I felt a glorious sense of exhilaration. Why, I was almost giddy!

This was the day Leonard discovered what cafeteria food really looks like.

Okay, I know we need to cut the budget wherever we can, but there has got to be a better way to create electricity.

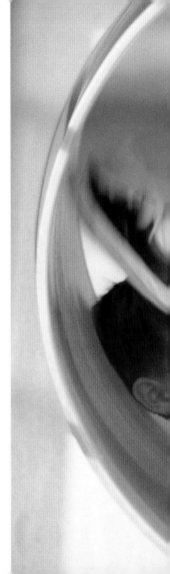

You'd think they were old enough to recognize a two-way mirror. At least that's what the school psychologist thought.

21

Those kids can swing around on that thing for hours without letting go. So why is it they can't hold on to a pencil?

The kids absolutely hated when I did it, but I refused to take their apples until they could find the state of Washington on the map.

Perhaps Jessie should consider the tambourine.

I said I'd be back in a couple of minutes—then I remembered they couldn't tell time yet.

Before I begin the first anatomy class of the year, I always check Mr. Bones. One year they turned his head around. Last year he had a hamburger in his ribs. Today he was wearing a wedding ring.

30

"Don't hush me, little boy. Just because you got this one right doesn't mean you know more than I do."

I bet the visiting doctor
can hear two hearts—
Carl's *and* the monster
that lives inside him.

When I heard
"It's your week for
lunchroom duty,"
I broke down and cried.

37

Does she really think I don't
know what she's been doodling?
Like I never put horns and a tail
on my teachers.

39

Mary Agnes aced the math quiz, but the only prizes I had in my desk were an almost-new toothbrush and a tangled ball of yarn.

One gift bag, a card, two apples, and a bouquet of flowers... do you think they're worried about parent-teacher conferences?

44

If you ask me, this is the definition of frustration. Every time he wrote the correct answer to the top problem, his shirt erased the answer to the bottom one.

Honestly, it was colored water. But since they were told it was alien ooze, they found science class a lot more interesting.

It's not the noise that gets
to me—it's the spit from
the spit valves.

Usually when a student has that pained look on her face, it means, "I have writer's block." I would have had more sympathy for her if she hadn't been looking through the window at the football players.

It's just not fair. You show them how to solve an algebra problem, and they're bored. Make one quarter disappear into thin air, and you're voted Teacher of the Year.

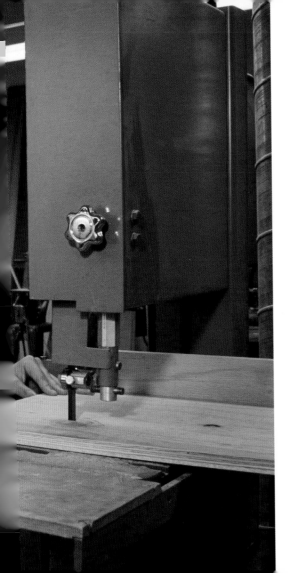

If every student has 10 fingers at the end of the year, I figure I've done my job.

It was the first time in my teaching career that every student wanted to contribute. Unfortunately, the discussion was about Saturday morning cartoons.

57

Sometimes students are transfixed by your illuminating lesson. Other times they're just trying to see how long they can go without blinking.

If I were given a choice between teaching preschool or teaching high school, I'd choose retirement.

These two apparently
haven't heard that
the principal is your "pal."

We went over it in class. I drew pictures on the board. I demonstrated with blocks. Yet somewhere between the classroom and the yard, the concept of "single file" completely vanished from their little heads.

65

Sure, Ms. Rodale is smiling now. But wait until the bus ride home when Kevin pulls out a fossil from the museum's priceless natural history collection and exclaims, "Look what I found!"

We had no idea what it was. All we knew was that we had to put it back in our teacher's desk before she returned.

Anne was thrilled,
but Zach balked when I told
him he'd be playing the lead in
Romeo and Juliet.

Students should never stick their heads out of a school bus window—unless, of course, that school bus is whizzing past a teacher getting a traffic ticket.

I knew it was going to be a long day when Stephen looked up at me and said, "Guess which hand has your car keys?"

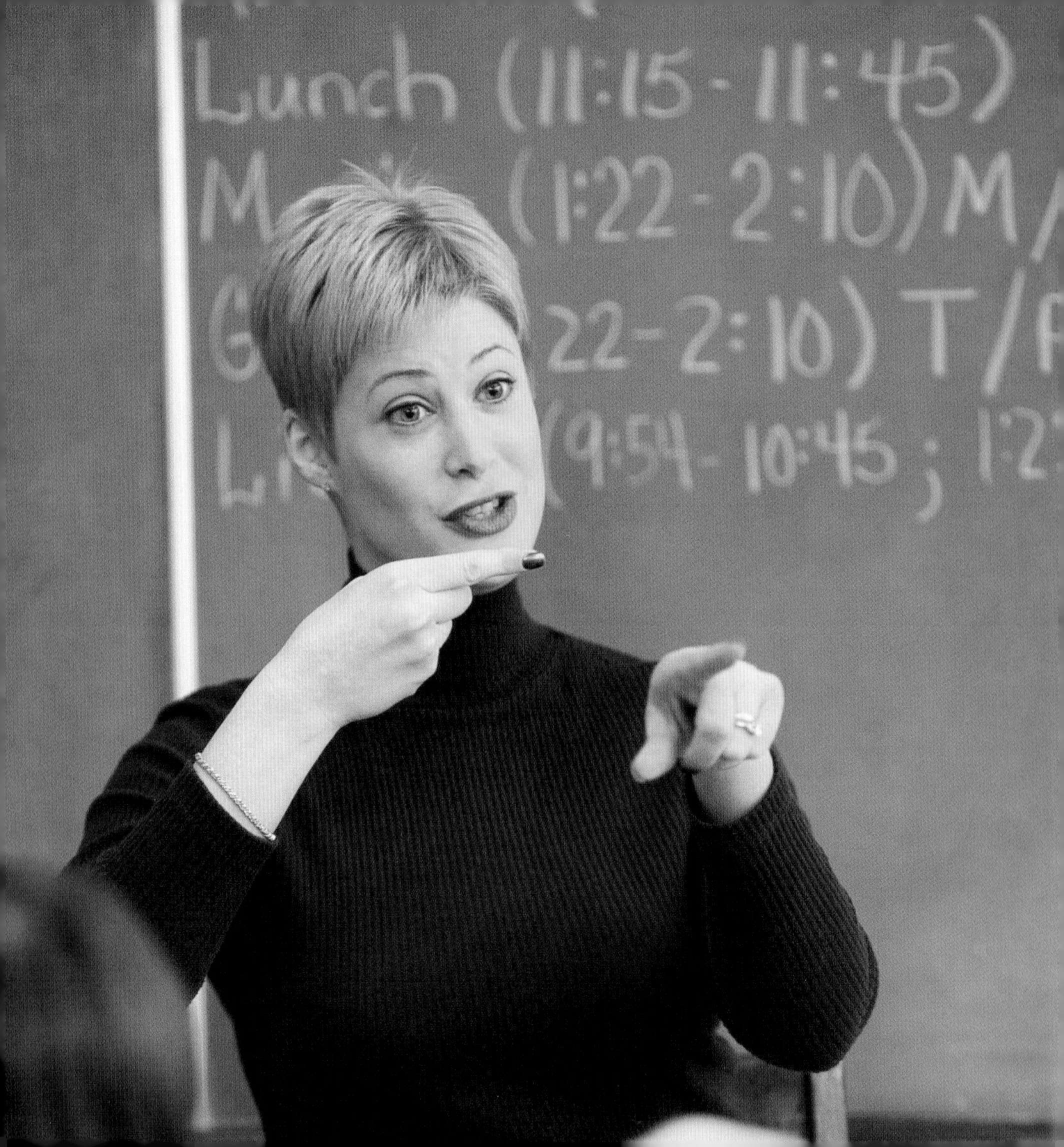
Lunch (11:15-11:45)
(1:22-2:10) M
22-2:10) T
(9:54-10:45;

I usually do it on the first day of school. The girls are never too impressed, but nothing gets the boys on your side quicker than explaining the velocity of a well-shot rubber band.